The Perfect Orphans Laws and Their Rights to Their Own Property.

Extracts from the Book of Creation

David Gomadza

www.twofuture.world

Copyright © 2024 David Gomadza

All rights reserved.

PAPERBACK: ISBN: 9798329091342

DEDICATION

Orphans' right to their own property without fear of being targeted and killed for their property.

CONTENTS

TABLE OF CONTENTS

THE PROBLEM 1   1
CURRENT ISSUES AND FINDING SOLUTIONS 2   2
FINDING SOLUTIONS 4   4
WHAT CAN BE DONE FROM AN ORPHAN'S POINT OF VIEW 8   8
108 RULES REGARDING ORPHANS AND THEIR RIGHTS TO THEIR OWN PROPERTY: EXTRACTS FROM THE BOOK OF CREATION 10   10
CONGRETE EXAMPLES AND THE FORMULATION OF RULES AND REGULATIONS 16   16
CHECKLIST OF QUESTIONS RELATING TO THE POLICE 18   18
FORMULATING OUR RULES AND REGULATIONS REGARDING ORPHANS LAWS AND THEIR RIGHTS TO PROPERTY 22   22
WHY ORPHANS ARE PERFECT FOR TO BE COLD CASES 33   33
THE PERFECT ORPHANS LAWS AND THEIR RIGHTS TO THEIR OWN PROPERTY 35   35
ABOUT DAVID GOMADZA 39   38

ACKNOWLEDGMENTS

A big thanks to Tomorrow's world order

THE PROBLEM

THE ORPHAN AND PROPERTY LAWS

laws that fight the death and property [dap] strategies of taking properties illegally from orphans
It is clear that the police have perpetrated a scene of death and property where they take property from orphans illegally and kill them in the name of capital gains tax collected for the monarchy but this law protects the police who end up taking the property themselves as in the cases we are looking at from the 1970s throughout to today it's a sad picture they are still doing it today a child was disposed and his name forced to be changed something we are against as Tomorrow's World Order we safeguard the rights of these orphans it is also Yahweh's duty as per book of creation.0892367890

CURRENT ISSUES AND FINDING SOLUTIONS

It is Yahweh's duty to everyone under the age of 16 then categorize these even further using an algorithm that defines those identified then ask a series of questions
1. What is
2. What could be
3. What is Yahweh
4. What can be
5. What is
6. What could be
7. What is
8. What is to be
9. What can be
10. What has been

Now if we look at all this then you can see that there are situations in life where there are other things in life in which things just happen for a reason but are already predefined that means when something is not as it is then it is a predefined parameter in which everything is within that time frame and must meet the conditions for it to work and if that happens then what can be of that situation if we look at the bottom line then there are chances that when things are not what it seems

The Perfect Orphans Laws and Their Rights to Their Own Property. Extracts from the Book of Creation

then there are not

Now let's look at this in the context of property and orphanage can we create a stencil that can be used to safeguard both interests without stealing and taking property then make it yours at the expense of women and children Yahweh defends the weak and will always take center stage and advocate for the orphans whose lives are destroyed needlessly and must be saved now if we look at all this from the point of view of the police they want capital gains tax before the property is sold in 99% of the cases we have looked at is this lawful if we look at this does this fall in the category of robbery of all the people they must know and act according to what are predefined rules and must only proceed if the previous check is satisfied that means we must put safeguards that make it impossible to proceed from one point to the other if we look at what can be done this is a possibility we can start by asking what can be of humans without the stealing police and those crooks who steal to benefit themselves things they took an oath to protect if we ask what can be done in this case then these are the solutions

FINDING SOLUTIONS

1. We can ask other independent bodies to complete one stage of the process this can be a bank or building society that can check ownership and make sure that all the rules are adhered to but only according to the predefined system parameters these must put signatures as well on the documents saying that the police have followed all the procedures and are acting within the law I think it is a bad thing for the police to take the law into their own hands if we look at this this way then you can easily tell that something is out of the ordinarily and will always be critical when deciding what to do in these situations if we are correct then we can say that we can always ask if you are doing the right thing because as predefined parameters we can always know when to start and stop this means that we can issue everything to everyone then go there and ask what can be done if nothing can be done then one has to ask oneself what can be done in these situations if nothing then we move on to the nearest point and ask these questions again until nothing can be done then we do the same so now to create such predefined stencils we need to understand the context in which all these occur most they occur under duress when a police officer start to admire

The Perfect Orphans Laws and Their Rights to Their Own Property. Extracts from the Book of Creation

property that belongs to others then that's a problem if we look at such a case we can look at the case that happened today in Canada where a police officer in the pretense of collecting capital gains taxes tricked a teenager to change her name today so that it's easy to claim back her house but in actual fact make it worse to claim back all this because he liked the house and has asked others to pretend to like the house so that there is bidding among the police this is the case between aspen ire who said today I got tricked by someone I trusted all my life for my own house that has nothing to do with the law but shear love of the property of others well-endowed in property I must change back this as soon as possible there are talks of God intervening everywhere so where is this God today I prayed all night to guide me but I did not hear him say anything there are stories in Mexico where God intervened and rescued a boy injured in the forest literally asking him to take away his pain and link him to his father even though the father turned out to be the enemy now if we look at this case then we can see the dirty tactics police use

1. They lie and unlawfully force the orphan to change his or her name just past 15 years old most on false or unsupported charges that make it unrealistic for orphans to deal with the law when about to claim the house if we look at this then we can always say if we look at this in this way then no kid can be tricked ever again we must include predefined settings in the system where both the police officer and the orphan involved are and must meet certain regulations to make sure that all is within the law the teen must always refuse and ask an independent body to stand for him instead before changing his or her name they make dirty deals because there are no safeguards to protect orphans from being tricked often with time frames for example nothing can happen at the same time

The Perfect Orphans Laws and Their Rights to Their Own Property. Extracts from the Book of Creation

the suggestion name change should be announce first followed by consultation by a third party and weeks later if within the law and all rules put in place for an automatic revert to original name 3 months before the collection of the house
This is critical because this will safeguard that when the house is due to be handed back then all the papers are in good form all names on identification documents matches those on the house
2. The police lie about the real reason for wanting the property all lie that it's to protect capital gains taxes if it's for capital gains taxes then they can't stay in that house this should be part of the predefined parameter in that they must not personally associate themselves with the property they are taking or their close friends in most cases they play syndicates in which they rotate the wheel of fortune and also rotate the turns for themselves and their friends this is easily avoidable by predefining this outright and have strict laws and punishment that says that if there is a problem then this is how to solve it now let's look at two critical issues regarding enforcing this
1. Police business is none of others business they are the only ones that can breach laws and still walk away in that by the time it might come to light of what is happening it might be too late you must always make sure that there are things that need checking as in ticking a box that can't be disclosed therefore there must be a third party to report to and turn to for clarification when the thieving policy decides that they want to take a property unlawfully if we look at what is happening in remote areas of Canada, Australia, England then you can see that the police have gone one step in the wrong direction targeting the rich and reduce them to rabble then take everything good they have to some even their money

The Perfect Orphans Laws and Their Rights to Their Own Property. Extracts from the Book of Creation

which they jam and force the bank to close the account and then try and withdraw the funds themselves now what can we do in such situations we can always ask what can be done and when then know what are our possibilities we can always ask other people to come to the rescue and take things to the better side we can always ask what is to be done then this is the answer we can always do what is right when it comes to things like asking the right questions if we are to proceed with this then what else must we look at and how is this so if we can then what can be done we must check all the possible options available then be ready to call for help if necessary if we look at what can be done then we can easily ask an independent advisor to verify everything we do we must be in a position to ask if there are things we can do then what are they and how can we accomplish these once that is answered then we can be ready to move on to the next step to make sure that there is nothing else we must do to make sure that the next stage is completed as fully as possible looking at all options once that is completed we can look at other things we must do to make sure that the orphan is fully aware of what must be done and how that can be done

WHAT CAN BE DONE FROM AN ORPHAN'S POINT OF VIEW

Now if we look at what can be done here are several options from an orphan's point of view
1. Ask an independent advisor
2. Request the presence of a second police officer who is not related to the one in charge
3. He can ask the bank to be his guardian and must sign documents as well checking everything that falls within the law
4. They can ask the building society or housing association what can be done and what to do next
5. They can ask the hospital to venture for them even though this is a risk but it might turn out
6. They can ask the doctor to vend for them and sign documents as well
7. They can ask the derelict property manager to sign documents as well because some use the derelict factor that the house can't be occupied because of damages then pretend to have fixed it at a huge cost then move in I mean literally moving in
8. If we look at this then what can be of the police who steal

The Perfect Orphans Laws and Their Rights to Their Own Property. Extracts from the Book of Creation

and jump the prison this is critical for the force to be trusted again stealing police officer must receive harsh treatment and always prison time this will make it a deterrent to others so that they can't steal again but what can be of these crooks they ought to be sacked with immediate effect anyone with a house obtained this way must return it by a deadline say 1.25 month after the announcement this is critical usually they ought to return within 6 months but we must as well quarter them to be fair to just 1.25 months this is Yahweh's predefined rules regarding this issue

108 RULES REGARDING ORPHANS AND THEIR RIGHTS TO THEIR OWN PROPERTY: EXTRACTS FROM THE BOOK OF CREATION

If we look at the book of creation there are 108 rules regarding this issue here are all the rules
1. Don't steal property that is orphans
2. Don't desecrate property owned by orphans
3. Don't intervene to disrupt ownership
4. Don't interfere for the sack of taking away
5. Don't ask others opinion as to cause disreputation among the orphans
6. Don't interfere to take rights from the orphans
7. Don't judge harshly orphan's trauma can cloud judgement instead give a helping hand
8. Never deposses an orphan no matter for what reason not even for capital gains taxes
9. Create a fund to help with bills and any costs within the society where the rich especially with oil are asked to vent for the orphans
10. Ask Yahweh for guidance using ask.ya.orphan

The Perfect Orphans Laws and Their Rights to Their Own Property. Extracts from the Book of Creation

11. Ask Yahweh for housing advice in regard to orphans using ask.housingadvice.orphan
12. Ask Yahweh for peace to orphan and among orphans
13. Ask what can be done regarding orphans everyday
14. What is to be of orphans and the law then this is the answer orphans are protected by laws under the sun meaning in every country orphans rights must be upheld throughout the world
15. Ask what can be of orphans in society this is the answer they can be of great help to society
16. What can be said of orphans with direction they can learn and live their lives peacefully and fruitfully
17. What can be of humans and orphans' orphans are people and must be treated with respect it's not a crime to lose parents
18. What is to be of housing and orphans there must be a strong relationship between orphans and housing
19. What can be said of orphans with wealth this is the answer they can start as leaders and end as governors who control great cities
20. What is to be of wealth and orphans everyone deserves a great opportunity in life and wealth is the starting point instead of stealing orphans housing they
must supplement their income instead of taking their property this is stupid to target the vulnerable to steal from them
21. We can always ask what is there between orphans and wealth there must be an intermediary to facilitate wealth and not hinder as current
22. What can be of wealth and other people other than God's people there are chances others respect orphans more than God's people
23. What is to be of orphans and society this is the answer

society must embrace orphanage and put in supporting structures that make sure that resources are channeled to orphans and to benefit orphans
24. If we are to ask today what can be of orphans and banks then this is the answer orphans can and must be respected by banks there must be a strong relationship between banks and orphans
25. If we are to ask what can be of orphans and money there must be structures that facilitates orphanage not as a burden but as part of society
26. We must address what causes orphanage in most cases it is also the police and the hospital behind this who can do harm than good so that they steal in the end
27. What is to be of orphans and the law they must be protected more laws must be put in place to protect often
28. If we look at what can be done then these are our options
29. Loan an orphan at reasonable market prices
30. Borrow the house and pay generously knowing that the person is an orphan
31. Regard all loans that can't be paid off by orphans as bad debt to be written off
32. Invent something and link it to orphans for patronage etc.
33. Employee orphans and hand generous pay package
34. Include in their article of association or memorandum generous terms knowing that they are orphans
35. Ask what can be done
36. Ask what could be of orphans and work
37. Ask what could be of orphans and work
38. Ask what is to be of orphans
39 Ask what is to be of orphans
40. Ask what could be
41. Ask what was and what can be

The Perfect Orphans Laws and Their Rights to Their Own Property. Extracts from the Book of Creation

42. Ask what can be of orphans
43. Ask what is to be
44. Ask what should be of orphans and the law
45. Ask what was and what is to be
46. Ask what is to be
47. Ask what can be
48. Ask what was
49. Ask what has been
50. Ask what if
51. Ask what has been but
52. Ask what is and what can be
53. Ask what was and what can be of orphans and the law
54. Ask what is and what can be
55. What is and what will be
56. Ask when and how
57. Ask what if but
58. Ask when and how
59. Ask what will be
60. Ask what is
61. Ask what would be
62. Ask when and how
63. Ask what if and what with
64. Ask what must and what is
65. What was and what will but how
66. Ask if we then what
67. Ask if we then with what
68. Ask what should be
69. Ask what can be
70. Ask what was what can be
71. Ask what will be
72. Ask what should be
73. Ask what was and could

The Perfect Orphans Laws and Their Rights to Their Own Property. Extracts from the Book of Creation

74. Ask when and how
75. What has been and how
76. What if and how
77. What is to be
78. What was and how
79. What should be
80. What must and will be
81. Ask what if and how
82. Ask what would be and how
83. Ask if not then what
84. Ask if not now than when
85. Ask what is but will not be
86. Ask if we then what
87. Ask what can be of orphans who are supported well
88. As what should be and when
89. Ask when and how
90. If not now then when
91. What is to be and how
92. What is to be and when
93. Ask what can be and how
94. Ask what if and when
95. Ask what was and how
96. If we start then what
97. What can be of a good network and orphans
98. What is to be of orphans with strong supported networks
99. What was and when
100. What should be and if not now then when
101. What must be
102. If not us then who
103. What must be of orphans
104. If not then when what how
105. If not now then when

106. What can be said of orphans with jobs can be fruitful members of the society
107. What was and can still be
108. What could be but is not yet

CONGRETE EXAMPLES AND THE FORMULATION OF RULES AND REGULATIONS

Now having looked at all these options now is the time to look at concrete examples and form possible rules and regulations
1. Add orphans in business directory
2. Ask for directions regarding orphans how do we deal with them
3. Ask what if and how
4. Ask what can be down and why
5. Ask what is to be
6. Ask what can be but
7. Ask what should be but
8. Ask if we are not then what
9. If not us then who to do it regarding orphans
10. What should be of orphans and society
11. What must be and could be
12. If not us then who
13. We must ask what can be of often with power
14. If not then what of orphans
15. What is to be of orphans
16. What was

The Perfect Orphans Laws and Their Rights to Their Own Property. Extracts from the Book of Creation

17. When was
18. What and when
19. What was to be
20. What should be
21. What can be of
22. What has been
23. What can be of
24. What should be
25. What was of orphans that can be again
26. What must be
27. What has been
28. What has to
29. What is to be
30. What should be

CHECKLIST OF QUESTIONS RELATING TO THE POLICE

If we look at all these other options you can see that now we are streamlining our response to be part of the solution now what is needed to do a checklist of the questions relating to the police if we are to ask what can be of others who are in that job can other people do the same and offend the orphans to such an extent to steal from them can doctors take properties that belong to the orphans can teachers take property that belongs to the orphans can soldiers take property that belongs to the orphans if not why then are the police in such a position to take and steal and as we have discovered kill as well if wives can kill their husbands who take the orphans property and kill them too then what can the president of the whole world do
This is what he can do
1. Enforce all current laws it is not that there are no laws its only that they are being broken
2. What can be of these laws depends on which ones are being broken
3. Ask what could be of orphans

The Perfect Orphans Laws and Their Rights to Their Own Property. Extracts from the Book of Creation

4. Ask what is to be of
5. What can be of
6. What was and can still be
7. Ask what has been and can be
8. What can be of orphans that can't be of others
9. What has been that can still be
10. If not now then when
11. If not us then who
12. If not them then who
13. If not these then who
14. If not those then who
15. If not us then who
16. If not these then who
17. What can be said of
18. What should be
19. What could be
20. What was What can be but not now
21. What is to be that can't be
22. What has to be
23. What should be
24. What can be
25. What was that can't be anymore but
26. What was that can still be but
27. What can be and how
28. What was and what can be
29. what is to be
30. If not now then what

If we look at all these questions a pattern start to appear all what can be done is nearly done but we can enforce and add eye witness to increase conviction which they count on as the hard but now we can use advance gadgets that tell everyone's thoughts and the brain at the same time the whole world

The Perfect Orphans Laws and Their Rights to Their Own Property. Extracts from the Book of Creation

meaning all secrets out for us to tell the truth and what is really happening that this is the only true future because of this many who think are above the law are going to fall because proof has never been more clearer than now that means now we take the case of aeropts and all the women he killed in Australia then the police are the ones who were behind the deaths and we have many confessing that they wanted to take the houses of a one Janine Vaughan and revelle balmain-smith confessing that it was their idea to get the women killed so that they can feast on their houses we have a series of gadgets we use that makes lying difficult and unavoidable now these are the instruments God uses and ones we use to prevent the police lying and intimidating orphans we record instant brain thoughts of every person on earth and test all against what is called the judgement test indicator what it does is to get a person his details and what he said throughout his life about anything and use this to find what he thinks and feels against other factors

We can also use an impedance that records everyone's thoughts and what they said at any given time and that measures many people at the same time

We can use other several ways to find out the truth like the geolocation mapping that identifies people within space and time to know their whereabouts and how and when they were there then use the impedance to get their thoughts after knowing their coordinates then know what they were thinking at that point in time

We can use a teleimpediance instead of just measuring and recording everyone's thoughts at any given time we can use a teleimpediance that records not just telephone lines but any communication between a lot of people I will give you an example there is a case about a drunken boy who decides to

The Perfect Orphans Laws and Their Rights to Their Own Property. Extracts from the Book of Creation

walk home after a night out then asked for a lift from a lorry driver then declined the lift after noticing sex toys then the lorry driver tracked back this boy on his way home and run him over this looks just like any other accident until you use our gadgets to find out that he was talking to a policeman who asked him to jump in one place instead of getting out of the way pretending to test his level of drunkenness instead the lorry driver thought he would jump and change position to out of the road resulting in the boy's legs crushed then after noticing this crushed him to death.

FORMULATING OUR RULES AND REGULATIONS REGARDING ORPHANS LAWS AND THEIR RIGHTS TO PROPERTY

Now that we have looked at all options we can now formulate our rules and regulations but first we must put things in place to make sure that the enforcement part is adhere to we must always ask all the questions to get the right answers and exhaust all until nothing is left unanswered then move to the next question this ensures that nothing is ignored and everything is looked at secondly we must make sure that these rules are enforceable and are adhered to thirdly we must always make sure that we address all critical issues regarding orphans all our rules and regulations must have orphans at heart this will ensure that all decisions to be made are in line with the needs of orphans and the protection they deserve.
There must be someone to oversee the work of the police and how they deal with them having said that I think it's time to write the rules we will use to make sure that orphans are protected.
1. Make sure there is a two-part signing system that addresses

The Perfect Orphans Laws and Their Rights to Their Own Property. Extracts from the Book of Creation

all our concerns from our investigations that the police
1. Trick orphans by changing their names so that claiming the house is difficult most of the cases we looked at how all have fake names which the police might use as an argument not to look at that case and class it as unsolved as the person does not exist for example revelle balmain-smith was tricked to change her name to just revelle balmain only to be killed a day before changing the name back in order to collect her house worth around 2million dollars
We have noticed that once the orphan has changed the name it's a trigger for death the police won't hesitate to ask someone to kill that orphan as changing the name give then added determination because the house will be within grasp with the orphan using another name this tells the thieving police that the house is free and within their grasp all they have to do is to get rid of the orphan and the house is theirs
2. Unlock all keys so that when a person signs documents they are locked so that no one else can see them with the added advantage that no one will know the name on the house. Once they know then they will start getting ideas to kill and rob.
3. Add additional features like a doctor, nurse, a bishop, a clergy etc. to sign as well on behalf of the orphan and to approve this is right. An elder that accompanies an orphan can give that orphan added support mind you why it's ease right now is the fact that a full grown up police man is dealing with unexperienced or uneducated orphans who they treat as kids and won't hesitate to steal from these but if a priest etc. is there then the policeman might not steal as he would have done if they were just the two of them document signing can be done in front of a third party a doctor, a priest, a nurse etc. as a deterrent also there must be added support for the orphan and networks to support the orphan

The Perfect Orphans Laws and Their Rights to Their Own Property. Extracts from the Book of Creation

4. Addition checks must be made regarding the police officer dealing with the orphans
5. There can be circumstances where the officer wants to trick the child then the child must have instruments to know what memory section he is using the brain tells us what memory is in use and this help the orphan know what is about to happen we have several memory modes but the most common ones are
1. Normal thinking
2. Brain memory where the brain takes over from the person and thinks
3. Thinking memory where the brain tells you what it is thinking and say it as words
Here the policeman can promise only as a response of the motive to steal
4. Imaginary memory is where you let the brain turn what you image into real action potentials
5. Inductive where the brain does things spontaneously
6. Intuitive where the brain does what feels good to it
7. Creative with tendency to lie to justify a reason where a person lies to support a genuine reason
6. There can be things put in place like an overseer who can stand for the orphan like a priest or clergyman
7. Laws that prohibit single police officers to approach orphans if that has anything to do with their house
8. Rules to forbid the seeking of capitals gains on houses that are not sold
9. Rules to stop policemen from getting houses once owned by orphans
10. Rules to ask what can be done about orphans
Askdotya what can be done
11. Rules to make police officers opt out of company housing

The Perfect Orphans Laws and Their Rights to Their Own Property. Extracts from the Book of Creation

to look for their own the police housing association to allow officer choices whether they want stolen houses or not
12. Ask rules to ban handing of all once orphan houses to the police housing association
13. Ban British laws that calls for capital gains taxes on houses owned by orphans.
14. Add other eyes like the doctors to monitor dealings with the police
15. Add resources to get other means of funding like an easy loan where loans are written off if not paid after certain times
16. Ask for new laws that asks why the policeman wants the house
17. Ask to add a justice system to report to that don't judge orphans outright but looks at the evidence then points fingers
18. Asks to unite everyone involved
19. All orphans who have houses must visit our website www.twofuture.world and download for free all software we use
a] we have a brain reader that lets you know exactly the real motive why the police man is asking you to change the house it tells you exactly why he is doing it without him knowing
b] we have an impedance that records every thoughts he has that records every thoughts of all people he contacts that whole day that records why he is doing this and what is his real motive all what the orphan needs is to say start stop at the beginning and let it record in real time every detail all everything within 500 meters radius
c] brain suspense this for 3 seconds suspense any persons brain to tell you a secret they are harbouring concerning you so this is all the orphans have to say
1. His or her name then that policemen brain will tell him or her his secret motive like he wants that house to live inside it

The Perfect Orphans Laws and Their Rights to Their Own Property. Extracts from the Book of Creation

to own it and sell it at a huge profit and all this first he must find a way to get you killed

2. It reveals his or her future plans regarding you today for example he will get you killed and hide all evidence so that your case becomes the hardest one to solve for 20 years and after that to collect the case reward money because he is the one who got you killed in the first place enough to solve that case

d] you can use a geolocation and a coordinates Identifier that tells you exactly where you are your electromagnetic wave and all details about that police officer

e] A translucence and transmitter is an instrument that records brain electromagnetic waves as thoughts words body movements etc. and sends all these to another person on the network or to a recording device this works well where an independent third party must be there but can't make it for example a priest or doctor or clergy they can get this and leave in the drawer of their office when they can't attend whatever happens between the orphan and the policeman is automatically recorded and sent to the doctors one so that all he had to do to know what happened is to play it so that everything said plays in your mouth and all brain thoughts in your own thoughts

F] the secret electromagnetic wave interrogator that works with codes everything you want to know from the policeman to check his credibility and motive you just ask this instrument and it will tell you everything say what you want to know as abbreviations

20. Ban on asking a deposit of only 20 dollars but to be in line with the current housing environment level

21. Ban quartering of capital gains taxes that leaves loopholes to be exploited the reason being that they withhold most of

The Perfect Orphans Laws and Their Rights to Their Own Property. Extracts from the Book of Creation

the money they would rather pay as capital gains taxes as they quarter the value first then calculate capital gains. That's means there are incentives to make millions in profit as the declared capital gains taxes are only a fraction of the quartered value once this is calculated and put aside in a file then the value is increased so that there are huge incentives to sell at a huge profit that mean crooked cops take life of orphans for rewards in millions when they sell the property.

22. Add an anonymous hotline to report thieving policemen without being identified to build trust and act as a deterrent to dodgy dealings and further channels to deal with intimidation after reporting a crook of a policeman

23. Set up a fund where donations are made and where oil rich countries are to help with funds for orphans where 50% of the money comes from the government etc.

24. Put in place very strict laws that punishes officer involved where the officer
1. Force or using tricks makes the orphan change the name not to match the name on housing papers
2. Where they take the house and the
3. orphan then end up dead.

We can argue that the force or trickery to change the name of the orphan is the first stage of a murder plan if these 3 conditions are met then it's a murder plan by the officer whether he is responsible for the actual killing or not.

25. Very strict punishment where it can be proved that they target orphans in order to create the cold cases that will last 20 years and give them work for 20 years where they just come to work and spend the day looking at the case and get paid but worse where they have killed orphans for the reward money which will top 1 million dollars after 20 years as they who have killed or made commands to kill an orphan and hid

The Perfect Orphans Laws and Their Rights to Their Own Property. Extracts from the Book of Creation

all the evidence for 20 years will not look forward to a million dollar retirement package where they don't give the reward on merit but to one of their syndicate players who collects the money just on behalf of all of them at least 21 other police officer players in the syndicate and deposit 90000 in each account and in his own account if something left then is deposited in the police housing association.

26. Ban police syndicate where they plan to get a free stolen house from orphans which they get by depositing 20 dollars only then help hide evidence over the years until the mature plan of 1 million dollars after 20 years and having raised a target of 8 million dollars where the 1 million dollars would come from leaving 7 million

27. Tough sentencing and immediate sacking without pay of officers in reward money killing syndicates where they expect a free house that they deposit 20 dollars only

1. They have killed 240 orphans so far and took their houses unlawfully for they had
2. Forced orphans to change their names so that claiming is hard
3. They had used codes to kill orphans, have used radiation to kill orphans, they have set up death traps for orphans for example starving the giant through hacking and control how he feels through tormenting to aggravate him enough to kill where he ended up killing those two women Janine and revelle balmain especially after confessing that they liked their houses
4. Then ignore critical evidence to solve the cases aiming for the 1 million reward after 20 years
5. Deliberately hides evidence so that the case becomes the most difficult to solve
6. Request evidence over 20 years at the beginning at 2, 5, 7.5, 10, 12, 17 and 20 years just requesting evidence in order to get

The Perfect Orphans Laws and Their Rights to Their Own Property. Extracts from the Book of Creation

rid of it

7. Twists evidence so that the case is unsolvable by switching evidence from one crime or from a drill used to distort the true events so that people won't know what happened

8. Distorting of evidence where over years to make sure that they have a tough case to solve then go on to create four possible situations to a case by

1. Looking for 3 other exact lookalikes and put four pictures of all different persons we suspect if you say I looked at the first photo thinking all are the same then they will show you the second photo of a living person most of the time you will have thought all photos are one person only to find out that the only photo you looked at the person is dead but the second photo which is that of a lookalike but totally different person according to electromagnetic waves is that of a different person who is alive

9. Falsifying of evidence by switch as to the crime scene where evidence of one crime scene is presented as evidence of a drill or similar case

10. Swindling government money deliberately where they know about the 1 million-dollar police syndicate designed to create 64 complex Unsolved Cases per cycle where they benefit financially holding secret accounts and expect refills every round where winners deposit money in all accounts

11. Laws to stop the causing of unnecessary sufferings among orphans through fist quartering of the house in order to calculate the lowest capital gains tax possible for the British monarchy and traumatizing the orphan through vandalism, sabotage and all kinds of bad things to reduce the value of the property and secondly use of deadly agents like cancer codes to kill fast breaking records of fastest killing agents with orphans having to see their vaginas fall while alive. No regard

The Perfect Orphans Laws and Their Rights to Their Own Property. Extracts from the Book of Creation

for orphan's life

12. Very tough sentencing including death sentence of police officers who ask doctors to secretly administer deadly poisons to kill orphans so they died on the date as calculated by their aty, asm etc. The sentencing is not regard to death per see but to the commanding of others to kill on behalf of them. This also punishes the giving of the license to kill orphans, quoting the saying that if I can then you can

13. Tougha sentencing for doctors who take advantage of the situation the lack of regard to orphans' life that they take things into their own hands and take this opportunity to test their own cancer drugs and experiment on them until death

14. Tough laws to protect the rights of single mothers with children and a house tough sentencing for those who try to use statistics falsely to victimize single mothers with house and write them as already dead that encourages others to think about testing their cancer drugs on them. The suggestion that singles mothers with houses die of cancer is in itself an injustice and there must be laws to discourage saying this in public. The main reason is that this suggestion leads to the next point

15. Targeted hacking of single mothers' children encouraged by the saying that single mothers with housing die early. This has meant injustices as children of simple mothers are now being hacked at birth to die just before they turn 22 This hacking is the one now being used to kill orphans as at birth a chip and a rotary propeller are inserted and the combination and the software is what is now being called aty or asm with mission to kill the orphan as its these they use to administer a lethal code or poison which kills orphans

16. Tough laws to deal with the unseen before cruelty towards orphans where the above chip and a rotary propeller are

The Perfect Orphans Laws and Their Rights to Their Own Property. Extracts from the Book of Creation

programmed to imitate a small boy or girl and are told that you must outsmart the human being and kill him or her and take his body. So that all these chips they call aty in Australia and asm in the USA and stupid in Britain all work to kill humans. Nowadays they have combined these with acetate that imitates humans to challenge and induce never seen before diseases like aggressive cancers where on birth it is fitted into the single mum parent child with aim to kill the mother with cancer as their saying that single mum's die of cancers because of stress but it's all deliberate. At birth the acetate in form of chip and rotary propeller will have the mission written already but saved as the last final page before shutdown

Task

I want everyone in the world with an aty from Australia, an asm from USA, a stupid from Britain, asy from Canada and azt from New zealand I want you all to say my voice is my password and ask your aty, asm, stupid and azt to read the last log file it will put at the end say let's read this file together. You will be shocked because its mission is to kill you and in 99.99999% of the time it has your day of death and the exact time and the time of day you will die until you remove it or fight this this is the day you will die.

But my main concerns are with the cruelty being employed when it comes to orphans. What these evils are doing is to program their aty, asm, azt, stupid etc. to be of the opposite sex and then give it a task to kill the orphan and take the body and to do a sex change operation before the orphan dies so when the orphan dies it will have also removed birth or her sex organs where they literally fall off.

This is what they are doing tell it [asm, aty, azt stupid etc.] to challenge humans in a game of wit and kill the orphan as fast

The Perfect Orphans Laws and Their Rights to Their Own Property. Extracts from the Book of Creation

as possible if orphan is a boy then the aty, asm, azt,qqa stupid etc. wants to be a girl that means just before death the orphan must also lose his genitals literally.

17. Tough laws against the police who kill orphans to invoke the wrath of God people over the years have tried to communicate with Yahweh [God] but with no luck because they look in the wrong places and use a totally different frequency God's frequencies is 13.8 Hzt what is happening now is this the police to test and see if God will come the last minute to ruin their 1 million dollar retirement reward package and ask them to return the stolen house the devised a plan to test and invoke Yahweh as if saying come today then we know you exist so that we know this reward plan and the syndicate are safe and will be ours after 20 years. Hence, they kill innocent orphans. In such cases there must be serious consequences for the officers involved.

18. Ban the police $1 million reward syndicate to take off the pressure to kill orphans in order to create a case that is so tough that it can't be cracked for the next 20 years. Cases with orphans are one of the most difficult to crack.

WHY ORPHANS ARE PERFECT FOR TO-BE COLD CASES

Orphans makes the perfect candidates for cases that can't be solved easily this is because:
1. Orphans can easily be made to disappear without a trace they don't have fathers or mothers who would offer money for their whereabouts.
2. Orphans can be replaced easily someone can easily kill an orphan and bring in a look like especially where they own houses.
3. Orphans trust the police more than any other group of people hence put all trust in the police the very people who will betray them
4. Lack of parents makes them vulnerable in that whatever they do in that the police can easily take advantage of that trust and make them sign forms to change their names easily after being tricked to on false account so that claiming the house is difficult
5. So far globally 240 orphans were killed and their houses were stolen by the police this is because they are weaker in

The Perfect Orphans Laws and Their Rights to Their Own Property. Extracts from the Book of Creation

dealing with life challenges

THE PERFECT ORPHANS LAWS AND THEIR RIGHTS TO THEIR OWN PROPERTY

Summary.aqqq

Legal and Regulatory Measures
Strengthen Legal Protections:

Property Laws: Ensure robust laws that clearly define the rights of orphans to inherit and own property. These laws should explicitly prohibit the unjust seizure of property.

Guardianship and Trusts: Establish legal frameworks for guardianships or trusts that manage orphans' properties until they reach adulthood, ensuring that these properties are protected from external claims.

Legal Representation:

Public Defenders: Provide access to legal representation for orphans, either through public defenders or pro bono services from law firms.

Legal Aid Organizations: Encourage the formation and support of non-profit organizations that offer legal aid to orphans and other vulnerable groups.

Regulatory Oversight:

The Perfect Orphans Laws and Their Rights to Their Own Property. Extracts from the Book of Creation

Government Agencies: Create or strengthen agencies responsible for monitoring and protecting the property rights of orphans. These agencies can intervene when there are disputes or allegations of wrongful seizure.

Ombudsman Services: Establish an ombudsman or similar independent office where orphans can file complaints and seek redress.

Community and Institutional Support

Awareness and Education:

Public Awareness Campaigns: Conduct campaigns to inform the public, especially orphans and their guardians, about their property rights and the procedures to protect them.

Education Programs: Implement educational programs in schools and orphanages to teach children and guardians about property rights and legal recourse.

Community Support Systems:

Community Watchdogs: Form community-based groups or committees to monitor and report any wrongful actions taken against orphans' properties.

Support Networks: Develop support networks involving local NGOs, religious institutions, and community leaders to advocate for orphans' property rights.

Administrative and Procedural Safeguards

Clear Procedures for Tax Collection:

Transparent Processes: Ensure that tax collection procedures are transparent and that there is clear documentation for any claims made against properties.

Appeals Process: Establish a straightforward and accessible appeals process for challenging tax claims or seizures.

Documentation and Records:

Centralized Records: Maintain centralized records of all properties owned by orphans, ensuring that any transfer or seizure of property is well-documented and can be reviewed.

Regular Audits: Conduct regular audits of property transactions involving orphans to detect and prevent fraudulent or wrongful actions.

Legislative Advocacy
Policy Reforms:

Lobbying for Change: Engage in lobbying efforts to amend existing laws or introduce new legislation that better protects the property rights of orphans.

Political Engagement: Encourage political candidates and leaders to prioritize the protection of vulnerable populations, including orphans, in their platforms.

International Standards:

Human Rights Frameworks: Align national laws with international human rights standards that protect the rights of children and orphans, ensuring compliance with treaties and conventions.

Collaboration and Partnerships
Public-Private Partnerships:

Corporate Social Responsibility: Encourage businesses to support initiatives that protect orphans' property rights through their corporate social responsibility programs.

Collaborations with NGOs: Foster partnerships between government agencies and non-governmental organizations to enhance the protection mechanisms for orphans.

International Support:

Global Networks: Participate in international networks and forums that focus on children's rights to share best practices and

The Perfect Orphans Laws and Their Rights to Their Own Property. Extracts from the Book of Creation

receive support for national efforts.

ABOUT DAVID GOMADZA

www.twofuture.world

The Perfect Orphans Laws and Their Rights to Their Own Property. Extracts from the Book of Creation

www.ingramcontent.com/pod-product-compliance
Lightning Source LLC
Chambersburg PA
CBHW030516220526
45464CB00006B/2825